I0397542

Simple Steps to Create and Launch Your Online Course in Seven Days

Dorcas Ayesu-Boahene

Published by Dorcas Ayesu-Boahene, 2019.

While every precaution has been taken in the preparation of this book, the publisher assumes no responsibility for errors or omissions, or for damages resulting from the use of the information contained herein.

SIMPLE STEPS TO CREATE AND LAUNCH YOUR ONLINE COURSE IN SEVEN DAYS

First edition. September 1, 2019.

Copyright © 2019 Dorcas Ayesu-Boahene.

ISBN: 978-1099867712

Written by Dorcas Ayesu-Boahene.

I'd like to dedicate this book to my dear husband, Nana Kofi Ayesu-Boahene, for always being there for me, I appreciate it, Sweetheart. To my first son Nana Kofi, for all the creativity, the long night stays just to edit and design my cover, you are amazing. To Papa Kofi, my second born for all the awesome titles you suggested, you are a genius. Oh, how can I leave my number one toddler editors, Aseda and Adepa, the distractions and continuous pressing on my keyboard spiced up this book. You all rock Dearies, and I love you to bits.

Special thanks to God for how far you have brought me. I could not have made it without you. I am forever grateful. To my mentors and various support groups, thanks so much for everything.

DEDICATION

I'd like to dedicate this book to my dear husband, Nana Kofi Ayesu-Boahene, for always being there for me, I appreciate it, Sweetheart. To my first son Nana Kofi, for all the creativity, the long night stays just to edit and design my cover, you are amazing. To Papa Kofi, my second born for all the awesome titles you suggested, you are a genius. Oh, how can I leave my number one toddler editors, Aseda and Adepa, the distractions and continuous pressing on my keyboard spiced up this book. You all rock Dearies, and I love you to bits.

Special thanks to God for how far you have brought me. I could not have made it without you. I am forever grateful. To my mentors and various support groups, thanks so much for everything.

INTRODUCTION

Why is Course Creation important for you right now?

- You have a tried and tested skill, but competition is not making you make money out of it like you are supposed to be.
- You have people that are yearning to learn your skill or trade but physical limitation and other barriers will not allow you to reach out to all of them.
- You wish you have a passive income that will be able to make you break free and let you live your life as you want

Now let's do this fast forward life to about 60 days from now – picture your skills bringing you good income that is guaranteed even whilst you sleep, vacate or take care of your family.

Do not worry about how you will get there, all I need from you is this

1. The right positive frame of mind

1. Determination

1. Delivering quality no matter what you do

1. Providing good value for money

1. Focus

And all that valuable skills you possess.
Are you with me?

MY AIM

- Is to show you the simplest way to create a course from your skills even though you have little or no prior knowledge in course creation.
- With little budget
- Then after the successful creation, to help you launch it successfully.
- This will take your income earning activity to a different level for you with no sweat, well just a little.

WHO AM I

I have been an entrepreneur for over 23 years now with a specialization in marketing I love mentoring and coaching people to realize their potentials.

I represented KNUST School Of Business, Ghana, and my alma mater, to compete in Manitoba, Canada, with only one other student, to win the enterprising award. This was done whilst managing the branch of a TV Station too.

To increase sales, I rebranded this branch of the TV Station during my tenure as the Branch Manager and successfully increased its revenue at that time by over 500%. I was in that position for over 12 years whilst doing other side hustles like creating documentaries and TV commercials for businesses.

After resigning, so I could take good care of my twins and other children, I created a niche that was new to my region. I was the first to open a grocery shop solely for children from 0 to 5 years. There were mother cares and other grocery shops with just a section for kids, but none of them was in this niche.

This business was born out of frustration in combing the whole town searching for consumables for my second baby. In the first year alone, I branded it so well that, I was making at least $10,000 a month from just one outlet.

I made many parents happy because I was not selling products to them, but benefits and was giving them free coaching on taking care of their babies.

Let me tell you one secret as to why I am so passionate about you focusing on your skills. Somewhere along the success lane, I tried to venture into other stuff apart from my skills in Marketing and Coaching. This nearly cost me my business, my reputation, and my hard earned money. Sales started dropping and I started going into debt. That was my reality check.

HOW DID THIS ONLINE course journey begin?

In February 2019, I was so frustrated with the situation I found myself in. In fact, at a point I had to put off my phone for a whole week just to keep my sanity.

In a bid to come out of the situation, I started spending a lot of time online trying to research on easy and quick ways to make money. Proof Reading, transcribing, virtual assistance, affiliate marketing, and many others.

Many eBooks and videos on YouTube promised and outlined a few gigs and jobs, but most of them were not accessible to those in Africa. The few that were opened to everyone, rejected my application to freelance because of my location.

I didn't give up. I joined mastermind groups. I believed this would help broaden my scope, if not to make money from a whole new area.

I was so delighted with this discovery because I know I can impart this knowledge to the others that are also aiming to make money online but don't know how.

So I aim at not just showing you how to market your skills alone, but rather give them the step by step approach to overcome those barriers. Sometimes all you need is the right niche, the right information, and the best way to market your skill to create a win-win situation.

My message to you is simple. It is time to focus on the skills that you already have, let people benefit from those skills, passion, and pay you for that.

You are a Graphic Designer, a Fashion Designer, a Caterer, a Beautician, a Dentist, Writer, Photographer, Instrument player, etc. The skill-list can go on and on. Did you know you can make good money out of it online? It does not matter your location, this can be done anywhere in the world

I don't want you making the same mistakes I did. People will come to you if you are offering them an opportunity to better their skills, acquire new knowledge and transform their lives. Don't think they will be competing with you when you teach them what you know.

You didn't re-invent the wheel, did you? The skills you have was imparted on you by someone. Even if you were born with it, you are not the only one who has that skill. Oh yes! If you do not impart it to people, others will do it and you will miss good money.

There is another twist here. You do not have to teach them your skill, but you can also teach them to benefit from what you do. For instance, a physical instructor does not have to teach someone to be an instructor but can have courses on exercises to better one's posture. A wellness expert can have courses on foods to eat daily to get rid of illnesses or correct imbalances in the body.

Do you get the drift?

Let's ask ourselves – What can I do so well and without much effort? What comes to me naturally? What skill have I perfected over time? You can write them in a notebook so you don't forget.

Now let's ask ourselves again? Is it something that people will be ready to pay for? What is the value tag placed on it? This exercise is important because sometimes you might be passionate about something, however, the demand for that service is so low that making it a business will not be advisable.

Now that we know our skills and are confident about them, let me show you one simple way that cuts across all Geographical areas, and will make you earn money even whilst sleeping or vacationing. That golden baby is **ONLINE COURSES.**

If we are ready and will psyche ourselves, then I can assure you that you will create your own course with these steps, in seven (7) days.

What do we mean when we say Online Course?

An online course uses the means of digital equipment to teach skills by providing them the necessary information needed to excel in that skill. This mode of teaching can take place anywhere in the world and it is not limited by geographical boundaries. All students need to access the course content is the Internet. He or she can decide to study on his or her phone, PC or Laptop.

Certificates are sometimes awarded to students after completion but most at times, these are dependent on the course provider or the market place where the course is being sold. A bit more details will come out in later chapters.

WHY AN ONLINE COURSE?

People are searching every day for ways to better themselves so as to excel in their chosen fields. However, their way of life or location will not allow them to go through the normal mainstream offline education. They, therefore, are comfortable if there is flexibility for them to be where they are and still upgrade themselves. This is where you come in.

You are an expert in your field and can impact this knowledge to those in need by providing them with needed knowledge at a fee. At the end of it, you benefit, they benefit, and it becomes a win-win situation.

There is the icing on this cake. You put in the effort once, you do it right, and you benefit from it for life. Whilst sleeping, vacationing or doing other things, you will be earning passive income from people signing on or enrolling in your course.

That is not all, you can gain more from your course through one-on-one coaching online from people who purchased your course but still want to be guided. A one- hour session can give you at least a $100.

Before we get to work, let me clear your mind from these myths.

MYTH 1

You need to be an expert before you can create an Online Course

That is not true. This is because you do not need special certification, a degree or a professional license to create one. The most important thing is to be on top of the skills you possess so as to be confident when teaching your students.

MYTH 2

You need expensive equipment before you can create Online Courses

This is another no-no that should be erased from our minds. No matter your budget, you can still create an online course and maintain the standard that is required at the market places for you to sell. You don't need expensive equipment before you can create Online Courses. When you can afford it, then, of course, no one will stop you

MYTH 3

Creating an online Course takes time

If you can create your course within seven days as I am about to let you do, then you will agree with me that it takes no time at all. Especially given the fact that you will make money from that little effort, throughout your life. You do not need to sell a perfect course but you need to provide a solution that will transform your student so much so that, she or he will rank you high wherever you go.

Now that our minds are cleared of these myths, let's move on to the main reason why we are here.

MODE OF PAYMENTS

Where do we start?

Knowing where we will be selling our courses is very important before we start the creation process. This is because different approaches are used depending on who will be hosting it. The 3 major places used quite often are Market places, Learning Management Systems sites, and one's own websites with the help of plug-ins.

No matter which one you choose you will still need an account for your revenues to be paid in. Signing up and getting your account confirmed takes a few days so we will take care of that first.

Well, we will be doing all the work we needed to done to make sure we launch our course, but how will we get the revenues we so much want? That is one major headache for people, especially those in Africa. I have therefore listed the supported countries for the 3 major payment gateways we are likely to use.

Go through, where you find your country is the gateway you would register with. If you find it in all three, I will advise you to choose either Paypal or Stripe. This is because most hosting sites and market places use the two so it broadens your market.

Payoneer is the alternative to the two above for Countries that are limited.

What this means is that your Geographical area will not be a stumbling block for your success, like I promised you earlier.

STRIPE Supported Countries

- Australia[1]
- Austria[2]
- Belgium[3]
- Canada[4]
- Denmark[5]
- Finland[6]
- France
- Germany[7]
- Hong Kong[8]
- Ireland[9]
- Italy[10]
- Japan[11]
- Luxembourg[12]
- Netherlands[13]

---

1. https://dashboard.stripe.com/register?country=AU

2. https://dashboard.stripe.com/register?country=AT

3. https://dashboard.stripe.com/register?country=BE

4. https://dashboard.stripe.com/register?country=CA

5. https://dashboard.stripe.com/register?country=DK

6. https://dashboard.stripe.com/register?country=FI

7. https://dashboard.stripe.com/register?country=DE

8. https://dashboard.stripe.com/register?country=HK

9. https://dashboard.stripe.com/register?country=IE

10. https://dashboard.stripe.com/register?country=IT

11. https://dashboard.stripe.com/register?country=JP

12. https://dashboard.stripe.com/register?country=LU

- New Zealand[14]
- Norway[15]
- Portugal[16]
- Singapore[17]
- Spain[18]
- Sweden[19]
- Switzerland[20]
- United Kingdom[21]
- United States[22]

PAYPAL SUPPORTED COUNTRIES

13. https://dashboard.stripe.com/register?country=NL

14. https://dashboard.stripe.com/register?country=NZ

15. https://dashboard.stripe.com/register?country=NO

16. https://dashboard.stripe.com/register?country=PT

17. https://dashboard.stripe.com/register?country=SG

18. https://dashboard.stripe.com/register?country=ES

19. https://dashboard.stripe.com/register?country=SE

20. https://dashboard.stripe.com/register?country=CH

21. https://dashboard.stripe.com/register?country=GB

22. https://dashboard.stripe.com/register?country=US

Country or region	Country or region code	Postal code
ALBANIA	AL	
ALGERIA	DZ	
ANDORRA	AD	
ANGOLA	AO	
ANGUILLA	AI	
ANTIGUA & BARBUDA	AG	
ARGENTINA	AR	Required
ARMENIA	AM	
ARUBA	AW	
AUSTRALIA	AU	Required
AUSTRIA	AT	Required
AZERBAIJAN	AZ	
BAHAMAS	BS	
BAHRAIN	BH	
BARBADOS	BB	
BELARUS	BY	
BELGIUM	BE	
BELIZE	BZ	
BENIN	BJ	
BERMUDA	BM	
BHUTAN	BT	Required
BOLIVIA	BO	
BOSNIA & HERZEGOVINA	BA	
BOTSWANA	BW	
BRAZIL	BR	Required

BRITISH VIRGIN ISLANDS	VG	
BRUNEI	BN	
BULGARIA	BG	
BURKINA FASO	BF	
BURUNDI	BI	
CAMBODIA	KH	
CAMEROON	CM	
CANADA	CA	Required
CAPE VERDE	CV	
CAYMAN ISLANDS	KY	
CHAD	TD	
CHILE	CL	
CHINA	C2	Required
COLOMBIA	CO	
COMOROS	KM	Required
CONGO – BRAZZAVILLE	CG	
CONGO – KINSHASA	CD	
COOK ISLANDS	CK	
COSTA RICA	CR	
CÔTE D'IVOIRE	CI	
CROATIA	HR	
CYPRUS	CY	
CZECH REPUBLIC	CZ	
DENMARK	DK	Required
DJIBOUTI	DJ	
DOMINICA	DM	

DOMINICAN REPUBLIC	DO	
ECUADOR	EC	
EGYPT	EG	
EL SALVADOR	SV	
ERITREA	ER	
ESTONIA	EE	
ETHIOPIA	ET	
FALKLAND ISLANDS	FK	Required
FAROE ISLANDS	FO	Required
FIJI	FJ	
FINLAND	FI	
FRANCE	FR	Required
FRENCH GUIANA	GF	
FRENCH POLYNESIA	PF	
GABON	GA	
GAMBIA	GM	Required
GEORGIA	GE	
GERMANY	DE	Required
GIBRALTAR	GI	
GREECE	GR	
GREENLAND	GL	Required
GRENADA	GD	
GUADELOUPE	GP	
GUATEMALA	GT	
GUINEA	GN	
GUINEA-BISSAU	GW	

GUYANA	GY	
HONDURAS	HN	
HONG KONG SAR CHINA	HK	
HUNGARY	HU	
ICELAND	IS	
INDIA	IN	
INDONESIA	ID	
IRELAND	IE	
ISRAEL	IL	
ITALY	IT	Required
JAMAICA	JM	
JAPAN	JP	Required
JORDAN	JO	
KAZAKHSTAN	KZ	
KENYA	KE	
KIRIBATI	KI	Required
KUWAIT	KW	
KYRGYZSTAN	KG	Required
LAOS	LA	
LATVIA	LV	
LESOTHO	LS	
LIECHTENSTEIN	LI	
LITHUANIA	LT	
LUXEMBOURG	LU	
MACEDONIA	MK	
MADAGASCAR	MG	

MALAWI	MW	Required
MALAYSIA	MY	
MALDIVES	MV	
MALI	ML	
MALTA	MT	
MARSHALL ISLANDS	MH	
MARTINIQUE	MQ	
MAURITANIA	MR	Required
MAURITIUS	MU	
MAYOTTE	YT	Required
MEXICO	MX	Required
MICRONESIA	FM	
MOLDOVA	MD	
MONACO	MC	
MONGOLIA	MN	
MONTENEGRO	ME	
MONTSERRAT	MS	
MOROCCO	MA	
MOZAMBIQUE	MZ	
NAMIBIA	NA	
NAURU	NR	Required
NEPAL	NP	
NETHERLANDS	NL	Required
NEW CALEDONIA	NC	
NEW ZEALAND	NZ	
NICARAGUA	NI	

NIGER	NE	Required
NIGERIA	NG	
NIUE	NU	Required
NORFOLK ISLAND	NF	Required
NORWAY	NO	Required
OMAN	OM	
PALAU	PW	
PANAMA	PA	
PAPUA NEW GUINEA	PG	
PARAGUAY	PY	
PERU	PE	
PHILIPPINES	PH	
PITCAIRN ISLANDS	PN	Required
POLAND	PL	Required
PORTUGAL	PT	
QATAR	QA	
RÉUNION	RE	
ROMANIA	RO	
RUSSIA	RU	Required
RWANDA	RW	
SAMOA	WS	
SAN MARINO	SM	
SÃO TOMÉ & PRÍNCIPE	ST	
SAUDI ARABIA	SA	
SENEGAL	SN	
SERBIA	RS	

SEYCHELLES	SC	
SIERRA LEONE	SL	
SINGAPORE	SG	Required
SLOVAKIA	SK	
SLOVENIA	SI	
SOLOMON ISLANDS	SB	
SOMALIA	SO	
SOUTH AFRICA	ZA	
SOUTH KOREA	KR	
SPAIN	ES	Required
SRI LANKA	LK	
ST. HELENA	SH	Required
ST. KITTS & NEVIS	KN	
ST. LUCIA	LC	
ST. PIERRE & MIQUELON	PM	Required
ST. VINCENT & GRENADINES	VC	
SURINAME	SR	Required
SVALBARD & JAN MAYEN	SJ	Required
SWAZILAND	SZ	
SWEDEN	SE	Required
SWITZERLAND	CH	Required
TAIWAN	TW	
TAJIKISTAN	TJ	
TANZANIA	TZ	
THAILAND	TH	
TOGO	TG	

TONGA	TO	
TRINIDAD & TOBAGO	TT	
TUNISIA	TN	
TURKMENISTAN	TM	
TURKS & CAICOS ISLANDS	TC	
TUVALU	TV	Required
UGANDA	UG	
UKRAINE	UA	
UNITED ARAB EMIRATES	AE	
UNITED KINGDOM	GB	Required
UNITED STATES	US	Required
URUGUAY	UY	
VANUATU	VU	
VATICAN CITY	VA	Required
VENEZUELA	VE	
VIETNAM	VN	
WALLIS & FUTUNA	WF	Required
YEMEN	YE	
ZAMBIA	ZM	
ZIMBABWE	ZW	

Courtesy: www.stripe.com

PAYONEER SUPPORTED Countries

Country Names:	Currency Names:
ALBANIA	Albanian Lek
ALGERIA	Algerian Dinar
AMERICAN SAMOA	United States Dollar
ANDORRA	Euro
ANGOLA	Angolan Kwanza
ANGUILLA	Eastern Caribbean dollar
ANTIGUA AND BARBUDA	Eastern Caribbean dollar
ARGENTINA	Argentine peso, Argentine austral
ARMENIA	Armenian Dram
ARUBA	Aruban florin
AUSTRALIA	Australian dollar
AUSTRIA	Euro
AZERBAIJAN	Azerbaijani manat
AZORES	Euro
BAHAMAS	Bahamian dollar
BAHRAIN	Bahraini dinar
BANGLADESH	Bangladeshi taka
BARBADOS	Barbadian dollar
BELARUS	Belarusian ruble
BELGIUM	Euro
BELIZE	Belize dollar
BENIN	West African CFA franc
BHUTAN	Indian rupee, Bhutanese ngultrum
BOLIVIA	Bolivian boliviano

Country Names:	Currency Names:
BOSNIA AND HERZEGOVINA	Bosnia and Herzegovina convertible mark
BOTSWANA	Botswana pula
BRAZIL	Brazilian real
BRITISH VIRGIN ISLANDS	United States Dollar
BRUNEI DARUSSALAM	Brunei dollar
BULGARIA	Bulgarian lev
BURKINA FASO	West African CFA franc
BURUNDI	
CAMBODIA	Cambodian riel
CAMEROON	Central African CFA franc
CANADA	Canadian dollar
CANARY ISLANDS	Euro
CAPE VERDE	Cape Verdean escudo
CAYMAN ISLANDS	Cayman Islands dollar
CENTRAL AFRICAN REPUBLIC	Central African CFA franc
CHAD	Central African CFA franc
CHILE	Chilean peso
CHINA	Renminbi
COLOMBIA	Colombian peso
COMOROS	Comorian franc
CONGO	Congolese franc, Zairean zaire
COOK ISLANDS	New Zealand dollar, Cook Islands dollar

Country Names:	Currency Names:
COSTA RICA	Costa Rican colón
COTE D'IVOIRE	West African CFA franc
CROATIA	Croatian kuna
CYPRUS	Euro, Cypriot pound
CZECH REPUBLIC	Czech koruna
DENMARK	Danish krone
DJIBOUTI	Djiboutian franc
DOMINICA	Eastern Caribbean dollar
DOMINICAN REPUBLIC	Dominican peso
EAST TIMOR	United States Dollar
ECUADOR	United States Dollar
EGYPT	Egyptian pound
EL SALVADOR	United States Dollar
EQUATORIAL GUINEA	Central African CFA franc
ERITREA	Eritrean nakfa
ESTONIA	Euro
ETHIOPIA	Ethiopian birr
FALKLAND ISLANDS (MALVINAS)	Falkland Islands pound
FAROE ISLANDS	Faroese, Danish
FEDERATED STATES OF MICRONESIA	United States Dollar
FIJI	Fijian dollar

Country Names:	Currency Names:
FINLAND	Euro
FRANCE	Euro, CFP franc
FRENCH GUIANA	Euro
FRENCH POLYNESIA	CFP franc
GABON	Central African CFA franc
GEORGIA	Georgian lari
GERMANY	Euro
GHANA	Ghanaian cedi
GIBRALTAR	Pound sterling, Gibraltar pound
GREECE	Euro
GREENLAND	Danish krone
GRENADA	Eastern Caribbean dollar
GUAM	United States Dollar
GUATEMALA	Guatemalan quetzal
GUERNSEY	Pound sterling, Guernsey pound
GUINEA	Guinean franc
GUINEA-BISSAU	West African CFA franc
GUYANA	Guyanese dollar
HAITI	Haitian gourde
HONDURAS	Honduran lempira
HONG KONG	Hong Kong Dollar (HKD)
HUNGARY	Hungarian forint
ICELAND	Icelandic króna
INDIA	Indian rupee

Country Names:	Currency Names:
INDONESIA	Indonesian Rupiah (IDR)
IRELAND	Euro
ISLE OF MAN	Manx pound, Pound Sterling
ISRAEL	Israeli new shekel
ITALY	Euro
JAMAICA	Jamaican dollar
JAPAN	Japanese yen
JERSEY	Pound sterling, Jersey pound
JORDAN	Jordanian dinar
KAZAKHSTAN	Kazakhstani tenge
KENYA	Kenyan shilling
KIRIBATI	Australian dollar, Kiribati dollar
KUWAIT	Kuwaiti dinar
KYRGYZSTAN	Kyrgyzstani som
LAO PEOPLE'S DEMOCRATIC REPUBLIC	Lao kip
LATVIA	Euro
LEBANON	Lebanese pound
LESOTHO	Lesotho loti
LIBERIA	Liberian dollar
LIECHTENSTEIN	Swiss franc
LITHUANIA	Euro
LUXEMBOURG	Euro
MACAU	Macanese pataca

Country Names:	Currency Names:
MACEDONIA	Macedonian denar
MADAGASCAR	Malagasy ariary
MALAWI	Malawian kwacha
MALDIVES	Maldivian rufiyaa
MALI	West African CFA franc
MALTA	Euro
MARTINIQUE	Euro
MAURITANIA	Mauritanian ouguiya
MAURITIUS	Mauritian rupee
MAYOTTE	Euro
MEXICO	Mexican peso
MOLDOVA	Moldovan Leu
MONACO	Euro
MONGOLIA	Mongolian tögrög
MONTENEGRO	Euro, Euro sign
MONTSERRAT	Eastern Caribbean dollar
MOROCCO	Moroccan dirham
MOZAMBIQUE	Metical
NAMIBIA	Namibian dollar, South African Rand
NEPAL	Nepalese rupee
NETHERLANDS	Euro
NETHERLANDS ANTILLES	Dutch guilder, Netherlands Antillean guilder
NEW CALEDONIA	CFP franc
NEW ZEALAND	New Zealand dollar

Country Names:	Currency Names:
NICARAGUA	Nicaraguan córdoba
NIGER	West African CFA franc
NIGERIA	Nigerian naira
NORTHERN MARIANA ISLANDS	United States Dollar
NORWAY	Norwegian krone
OMAN	Omani rial
PAKISTAN	Pakistani rupee
PANAMA	United States Dollar, Panamanian balboa
PAPUA NEW GUINEA	Papua New Guinean kina
PARAGUAY	Paraguayan guaraní
PERU	Sol
PHILIPPINES	Philippine peso
POLAND	Polish złoty
PORTUGAL	Euro
PUERTO RICO	United States Dollar
QATAR	Qatari riyal
REUNION	Euro
ROMANIA	Romanian leu
RUSSIAN FEDERATION	Russian Rouble (RUB)
RWANDA	Rwandan franc
SAINT KITTS AND NEVIS	Eastern Caribbean dollar
SAINT LUCIA	Eastern Caribbean dollar

Country Names:	Currency Names:
SAINT PIERRE AND MIQUELON	Euro
SAINT VINCENT AND THE GRENADINES	Eastern Caribbean dollar
SAMOA	Samoan tālā
SAN MARINO	Euro
SAO TOME AND PRINCIPE	São Tomé and Príncipe dobra
SAUDI ARABIA	Saudi Riyal
SENEGAL	West African CFA franc
SERBIA	Serbian dinar
SEYCHELLES	Seychellois rupee
SIERRA LEONE	Sierra Leonean leone
SINGAPORE	Singaporean Dollar
SLOVAKIA	Euro, Euro sign
SLOVENIA	Euro
SOLOMON ISLANDS	Solomon Islands dollar
SOMALIA	Somali shilling
SOUTH AFRICA	South African Rand
SOUTH KOREA	South Korean won
SPAIN	Euro
SRI LANKA	Sri Lankan rupee
SURINAME	Surinamese dollar
SWAZILAND	Swazi lilangeni, South African rand

Country Names:	Currency Names:
SWEDEN	Swedish krona
SWITZERLAND	Swiss franc
TAIWAN	New Taiwan dollar
TAJIKISTAN	Tajikistani somoni
TANZANIA	Tanzanian shilling
THAILAND	Thai baht
THE GAMBIA	Gambian dalasi
TOGO	CFA franc
TONGA	Tongan pa'anga
TRINIDAD AND TOBAGO	Trinidad and Tobago dollar
TUNISIA	Tunisian dinar
TURKEY	Turkish lira
TURKMENISTAN	Turkmenistan manat
TURKS AND CAICOS ISLANDS	United States Dollar
TUVALU	Australian dollar, Tuvaluan dollar
UGANDA	Ugandan shilling
UKRAINE	Ukrainian hryvnia
UNITED ARAB EMIRATES	United Arab Emirates dirham
UNITED KINGDOM	Pound sterling
UNITED STATES	United States dollar
URUGUAY	Uruguayan peso
UZBEKISTAN	Uzbekistani so'm

Country Names:	Currency Names:
VANUATU	Vanuatu vatu
VATICAN	Euro
VENEZUELA	Venezuelan bolívar
VIETNAM	Vietnamese dong
VIRGIN ISLANDS (U.S.)	United States Dollar
YEMEN	Yemeni rial
ZAMBIA	Zambian kwacha
ZIMBABWE	United States Dollar, South African rand, Euro, Renminbi, Indian rupee, Pound sterling, Botswana Pula

Courtesy Ezbing.com

The links below will get you to their website for the signup. You should have your ID, Address, Bank account details including Swift Code and Sort Code (Easy to get online if you have your bank name and branch), when signing up. They will be needed no matter the one you choose. So if we are ready, let us do it now.

www.stripe.com[23]
www.paypal.com[24]
www.payoneer.com

---

23.   http://www.stripe.com

24.   http://www.paypal.com

WHERE TO SELL OUR COURSES

Now that we have our payment accounts set up, Let us know what these various hosting sites and Market places bring on board.

1. ONLINE COURSE MARKETPLACES

These are platforms created for students to enroll in all types of courses. They make selling easier for course creators because they do all the marketing for courses they sell. Most students also know them already and trust them so they give more credibility to courses. There are many of these platforms but as a beginner, I will recommend UDEMY.

Below are some of the reasons for my choice:

a. Udemy has the easiest way of entry for both Instructors. After verification of identity, the quality of your course will decide on whether you can sell it here. If you followed all my steps, then we don't have a problem with quality.

a. You determine your own course price using their range as a guide. However, when there is a promotion ongoing, UDEMY can decide to slash your prices for more students to enroll. The maximum to price is $50 now but most at times, all courses on UDEMY are sold between $10 to $20. They are always running discount promos to drive traffic to their site.

a. It is free to upload your course on UDEMY. They make money by promoting and selling your courses for you. They take 50% of the revenue that comes in. Where you get affiliate revenues in addition, they will take 25% of that. You, however, get to keep 97% of your revenue when you promote your courses yourself and sales come out of that. I think that's cool looking at the fact that it is more of a passive income once you have uploaded it. All it takes is updates from time to time.

a. Students love UDEMY too, from figures generated by researchers. They have the highest number of students so far as compared to other market places for online courses. Why won't they love it, you buy a course and have access to it for life. Unlike other places where you have to subscribe and pay monthly.

b. UDEMY will do your marketing for you and that is a big deal. You cannot be noticed without marketing no matter how good you are. Not just in online courses but for any venture you embark on.

UDEMY pays you through Paypal or Payoneer. You choose the mode of payment when signing up.

1. SELLING COURSES ON LEARNING MANAGEMENT SYSTEM (LMS)

Marketplaces present an easier option but you have no control over pricing your course. All courses virtually are sold for between $10 to $20, on UDEMY. The benefit comes from the quantum of students that enrolls. You also have no control over student information and so you cannot build your email list from there.

Owning your own website and hosting your courses might also be too overwhelming for you. To overcome these challenges without losing out on the advantages with UDEMY, ready-made platforms have been created by Companies. Technology has advanced so much so that, with just a few clicks and a few minutes, you can have a full functioning hosting site for your course, customized to suit your brand, without being a technical person, yes.

Well, we will part with a few dollars to get that either from sales or through subscriptions. These are referred to as **the learning management system (LMS)**

This is how Wikipedia defines it, "A **learning management system (LMS)** is a software application for the administration, documentation, tracking, reporting, and delivery of education courses, training programs, or learning and development programs". It simply means it is a software that creates an online course, delivers it, and reports on activities that go on.

It presents to you a typical classroom setting but without students physically seated. You are able to enroll, monitor students by quizzes and even know where each of them has reached in the syllabus. The icing on the cake is that depending on the plan you pick, you can even award your own certificate.

A learning management system gives you all the necessary tools to upload your course whether in bits or all at a go. Providing you with all the necessary security you need to ensure your course, as well as your revenue, is well protected. It allows you to customize in line with your brand.

It makes online course creation simple and easy to promote and sell. It gives you the authority to price, promote and do other things. You have control over your students' information, unlike the marketplaces. You can use these platforms to funnel your paid courses and even host other authors.

A typical example is Thinkific.

Thinkific is a Canadian owned cloud-based Learning Management System (LMS). It has a free plan for Beginners and subscriptions for individuals and organizations that want more.

When you sign up for the free plan, they take 10% of your sales. However, with this plan, your students will not be given completion certificates.

There are other limitations but as a beginner, this might not really be a big deal as it represents our best interest because we have no budget to spend at the moment. We can opt for their other plans for more benefits when we advance.

Mode of Payments for Thinkific

Thinkific pays you through Paypal or Stripe, and you are paid instantly when a purchase is made. The choice of payment gateway to use will come from you.

1. SELLING FROM OWN WEBSITE

Another way for you to sell your courses or to get students enrolling is to do so through your own website.

To do this, you must have plugins and security features that will ensure that you are not handed a raw deal by hackers and other bad nuts. As a beginner, this will be quite daunting.

There are however a lot of videos on you tube to guide you through a simple set up with all the plug in available for a fee. That is the landing page set up, the payment integrations etc.

The first step is to get a domain name, I used Name Cheap after reading several reviews. Then you get a business hosting site. Again after reading several reviews, I went in for In Motion. Blue Host is another good option but they tend to be a bit more expensive. They all come with an SSL Certificate which is very important for the security of the website.

I bought the domain name and the rented the hosting site, then because I had a lot to do before my launch date, I contracted a web developer to do the rest and gave him a list of things to do. Their services are expensive at some places but it is a bit affordable from where I come from without compromising on your security.

You can get in touch if you have any difficulties.

You can use all three payment gateways or one depending on which one is accessible to you.

Ok, now that we know all the three avenues we can use, the choice is ours. If we can only use Payoneer, then UDEMY will be our best option for now and later we can set up our own website too for control.

BEFORE WE START CREATING

You may have attempted some things and failed like I did, or might have succeeded as I did too. However, no matter what happened, we are here because we want more in life. There is this popular saying that in spite of the sea having so much water, it still receives water when it rains. This simply means no one can say he or she has so much money that she doesn't need anymore.

We can create great courses within days when we set our minds to it and follow the right approach. By the time we get to the end of this book, we should be better placed to finish ours as soon as possible. Time waits for no one and the simple approach that I will teach you will get your course created easily whilst maintaining its quality. Don't be scared, longer times do not guarantee better quality.

Sounds great, right?

With us agreeing that we will use UDEMY to launch our first course,

Let me give you the minimum requirements for a course to be published on their website. As a beginner, this will guide us and will be a good benchmark no matter where we want to sell our course.

- At least 30 minutes of video content

- At least 5 separate lectures
- Valuable educational content
- HD video quality (720p or 1080p)
- An Audio sound that comes out of both channels and is synced to video
- Audio quality that is not distracting to students

When people click on your course or are led to the front page of your course, that is the landing page, UDEMY expects these points to be clearly stated there

- A high- quality course image in-line with Udemy image standards (min. 2048x1152 pixels)
- A well-written course title and subtitle that includes relevant keywords
- A brief, honest, well-written course description
- Clear course goals, target audience, and requirements that are easy and understand
- A credible and complete instructor bio and profile picture

Sounds like too much to swallow? Don't worry, I am here to guide you through every step of the way to ensure you master all the needed requirements before we publish our first course.

Good, it is time to know the different modes of presentation so we can arm ourselves before we begin.

There are different ways you can use to make sure your lessons are engaging to your students. This most at times are dependent on the lessons you are treating. As much as a beginner will want to hide from the camera, a skill demonstration may be such that the only way your student can grasp what you are teaching will be to show yourself in the process.

Let me take you through the modes and guide you to pick the best based on your specialty and target.

i. Slides with voice over

Slides are text typed boldly in either PowerPoint or with the help of Google's software. This is good for beginners especially if this is the first time you are trying your hands on such a venture. This mode requires little capital and so you can create your own courses without thinking of where you can get money to start. You can still get the quality in audio and text for you to stand out.

For this mode, you do not need an expensive camera, and an expensive microphone or an expensive editing suite. It, therefore, breaks that myth of online courses being expensive.

If you are camera shy, then this option is for you till you gather your momentum and confidence to face the whole world. I know, right? That's the beauty of the internet.

This mode allows you to send your tutorials across without showing your face. In this case, students are not distracted by you. They can concentrate on what you are saying. Research shows that students absorb better when they listen and read at the same time.

The other advantage is that with the busy lifestyles we have now, your students can still listen on-the-go without worrying about your expressions.

Let me add that sometimes the skills you are teaching will not permit you to use this mode.

Now let's look at the other presentation formats;

i. Slides with video.

This type needs more work but it gives your student the chance to connect with you and see how confident you are in teaching what you love to do. It is less boring and is good for courses that include demonstrations.

Here, you will be seen on one part of the screen whilst your slides will occupy the other part. It can be on one side or under your image. You could also alternate between the slides and you. They all work well. This mode requires you to stay focused on the camera and you should look good in camera. It requires your confidence. If you are fidgeting whilst teaching, then it is another way of saying they should not trust you and whatever that you are saying.

The secret to this is to imagine yourself having a one-on-one chat with your student or friend. That will make you come out interesting and more engaging. I love the conversational style of communicating because it builds trust and confidence. It makes you come out friendly and warm to your students.

i. FULL VIDEO COURSES

This is where the most work is needed. Your location, sound, camera, and lighting will all have to be on point. It is used for advanced courses and with courses that require full demonstrations and full student engagements. Here, let me emphasize that your location is very important. If your course is on baking, then your background should reflect it. A neat well organized set is a must if you want to be taken seriously

TOOLS TO USE

What are the tools needed?

Laptop – This is your money-making machine. Take good care of it for me. You will need it from Day-1 till you become a millionaire, and beyond.

Notepad or word – this is the tool to organize all your thoughts, ideas, research. I use my Samsung note, Microsoft word and a small notepad that follows me wherever I go. The latter is very important because sometimes something will come to mind that you will want to add to your course. Your laptop will not be handy but you may have your phone or your notepad. There and then, you write it down so you don't forget. It doesn't matter if you have published your course already, you can still update. That is the beauty of digital courses. You can update whenever you want based on a change in some methods or upgrades that will benefit your students.

Internet connection – Yes, sometimes whilst in the process of creating, a thought will come to mind again and an image may be needed to bring that thought to life. Other times, it might be a confirmation of a thought or expert advice that you would need online. Internet connection is actually the heartbeat of online entrepreneurs. We eat with it, work with it, play with it and even sleep with it. Funny but true.

Microphone

Audio quality is very important because, without that, most online course marketplace will not host your course. Outside of that, people will sometimes be listening to you on a browser whilst doing other things. They, therefore, will require you to give them the best of audio. All they need is no interference from the background whilst listening to you. For this, we will have to use an external microphone. By this, I mean a microphone that is not in-built with your laptop. If you are using your phone's voice recorder, it should be set to the highest quality. The reason is that you can adjust it to the way you want to make it sound better. The best position is under the chin and closer to the mouth. All microphones sound better when it is closer to your mouth, and with this mode, there is no fear of it appearing in camera.

If you would use the slide with video or the full video option, then you would not want to distract your students. So a microphone that can be concealed is ideal.

You can also use that of a good smartphone but it should be outside of the camera range. I use both my smart phone voice recorder sometimes. Other times too I use the audio of my Logitech HD Webcam. They all work perfectly well

There are innovative ways of getting the background noise taken out. This can be done with a simple box to get the mic closer to you as possible, then a big towel to take out the echo by dampening the sound. The towel should be folded and placed on top of a box before positioning the microphone. Or after recording you can use Audacity to do edit the background noise out.

Then again if you find that too much of a task, contract someone from Fiverr to do for a fee. You can get more tutorials and resources from my website. www.simplestepsseries.com[1]

---

1.   http://www.simplestepsseries.com

https://sscoursecreationschool.teachable.com/p/home

HD WEBCAM OR A GOOD quality HD camera

If you don't have any, a good smartphone with an HD camera can be used initially till you make some good sales.

LIGHTING

Ideally, 2 pcs of 18inch paper lanterns 105 watts 6500k bulbs will be best for lighting. However, you can make do with any good light, but these options are available for you. For you to be seen well with no shadows, your lighting around your set up should be looked at.

HOW TO GET A SIMPLE set up right in your home or office for the in-camera presentations:

Your HD Webcam should be attached to the top of your PC or Laptop. This laptop or PC must have been positioned on the desk already, with no clutter to distract. You can also mount it on a tripod if you have any or a selfie stick but with something to hold it in place. If you are using your phone, please remember to put it in flight mode during the recording process.

Your lights should also be positioned in such a way that it gives you even brightness with no shadows but out of the camera range. This will give you even lighting on the face whilst you look directly into the camera. You will definitely know if there are unwanted shadows. Adjust the position till you get the best.

Your background can be changed with any color at all or a custom image that you prefer. I will show you how to do it during the editing process.

Like I explained earlier, the best place for your microphone should be below your chin, and outside of your camera range. However, if you are using a cordless microphone and it is small, then conceal it neatly in your shirt or dress.

As you become more advanced and well placed to invest more money, setups can be varied to include more equipment.

It is important to note though that the modes of presentation sometimes overlap in one way or the other as we become more advanced in our presentations.

NOW THAT WE KNOW THE different types of modes we can adopt for our course now, and we also have gathered the needed tools, it is time to proceed.

Before we do that though, let us get a bit practical here. This link will take us to UDEMY but this time to find out the best video and audio qualities acceptable. We wouldn't want to waste our time creating our course only for it to be flagged down because of errors that could easily have been avoided. Don't worry, this will only take a few minutes of your time but it is worth every bit of it.

https://www.udemy.com/share/1006b8B0sceFhWRnw=/

Now let's move to another important segment

EDITING TOOLS

Your course will stand out with the best of editing.

Screencasting screen recording software is one of the most useful tools to fall on when you want to create an online course. Whether you want to record your powerpoint or google slides as you will learn to do. Or you want to explain things on your computer screen visually, you will still need it.

It gives you the opportunity to record along with the audio. This can include your voice. You can also record with your HD Webcam, recording yourself whilst shifting between what is on your screen and talking.

However, as a beginner, some editing software can be intimidating. That is why I will advise you to go in for good editing software that is friendly to beginners. For the sake of a tight budget, however, I will still list the free tools here, and the ones that are affordable

Below are some of them. I have indicated those that are free and those that are not.

<u>Audacity</u>

- It has been tagged as the best free software for recording audio. If you used a microphone, Audacity can record the live audio from it and even from other media too. It can import, edit, and combine sound files.

- With this software, you can export your recordings in different file formats even with multiple files all in one go.

- It is easy to use for editing with the simple Cut, Copy, Paste and Delete. You can go back to correct your errors with just simple undo, redo, etc. in the session to go back any number of steps.

<u>SCREENCAST O MATIC</u>

This costs between $2 to $4 a month. The deluxe option is the one with all the benefits and I will advise you to go for that, and it is far cheaper than most of the other editing tools but will do the work equally with just a little effort.

- It allows you to record your screen if you need to demonstrate something, including your webcam shots if need be.

- Audio recording and editing ability

- Video recording and editing ability including

background change and picture-in-picture.

- Secured Cloud storage whether on your website or other platforms

OTHER TOOLS THAT COME handy are:

GOOGLE SLIDES:[1]

- This is also a free tool, great for making your slides. Google Slides brings out the best in your presentations with a variety of themes, many font styles, embedded video, and animations, all without paying a single cent.

- They have many portfolios, pitches, and presentations already made to make your course look great without much effort.

- You can have access to create and edit your presentations wherever you may be when you install the Google Slide App installed on your phone, tablet, or computer. This can even be done without an internet connection.

- You can convert from Microsoft PowerPoint files to Google Slides and vice versa.

---

1. https://www.google.com/slides/about/

<u>PowerPoint</u>

PowerPoint plays similar roles as Google Slides

<u>Pexels/ Freepik</u>

Provides you with free images to bring your presentations alive. You might be talking about cupcakes but needs very good images to back it up. You can get some from this site for free. Remember copyright issues are very serious so it is important to work with images that are free to use and without any brandings from the owner. This is where these two sites come handy.

EASYVSL SOFTWARE also makes course creation very easy. This software has all the above embodied in one. However, you need 97$ to enjoy the benefits and 10$ every month as a subscription.

Below are some features as listed on their website to help you take a quick decision.

- Instead of manually typing on the slides and adding up as you go along, you just put the transition icon (they will show you if you pick this software) in front of where you want the slides and it will create it for you.

- These slides come with different styles and colors that you can choose from to add beauty to your course appearance.

• If however due to branding, you will prefer your own custom template for your slides, you have the option to upload your own.

• EasyVSL can automatically sync your entire voiceover audio to your slides... transitioning the slides at the perfect time. This is done using their built-in speech recognition and intelligence feature, This means you do not have to manually sync Your Video Slides with Your Voiceover Audio!

• Allows you to Insert Existing Video Clips - This feature is perfect if you picked the slides with video or the full video as your option.

• Text-to-Speech (TTS) - Don't want to record your own voiceover? Not a problem! Choose one of their natural sounding voices to read the text on each of your slides, creating an audio file that can be used for your video. (I will advise you don't use this feature though, use your own voice to register how authentic of your course is)

You get instant access to over 1,000,000 royalty free images/graphics directly from inside EasyVSL, for an easy way to enhance your videos. Or you can upload your own ones.

• Simple-to-Use Timeline Editor

- Export Slides to PDF Presentation

NOW YOU HAVE THE ABILITY to export your EasyVSL slides into a PDF, so you can share them with others or use for a presentation.

- 1-Click Translation

Marketing to several different countries? Instantly translate your text using our built-in translation tool. In just a few minutes, you can create multiple videos, specific to the language of your choice!

- You can export your videos in various mp4 qualities from web-ready, all the way to HD.
- 1-Click Video Syndication

Once your video is created, now it's time to share it with the masses. Now you publish your videos to popular video sites like YouTube, Vimeo, and many others from directly inside EasyVSL.

- You can also install EasyVSL on multiple computers.

While most software only allows one or two installs. With EasyVSL, you'll be able to download and install it on up to 5 computers. EasyVSL is both PC and Mac compatible. After you order, you'll be directed straight to the download page. You'll also be emailed download instructions so you can easily install it on additional computers you might own.

Courtesy: www.easyvsl.com

FAIR DEAL, RIGHT?

Alright, nothing stops us now from creating our course.

THE PROCESS

L et's identify your passion –
       DAY 1/ STEP 1

For your targeted customer to fall in love with you, you need to prove to them that you are good at the topic you are treating. Let them know that you are the go-to-brand because they will get value when they come to you.

To be very sure about this, list all the things you are good at- Is it the use of excel? Word? Playing an instrument? Organizing events? Copy Writing? Baking, Hair plaiting? Kids Care? Elderly Care? This list can go on and on. Pick a paper and list all the things you can do and do well. Without being passionate about it, you will come out boring and your confidence level will be low and you will suck, so please list things you are comfortable with and do well. This is because this course can propel you into greater heights where you will be called for one-on-one coaching. Well, if you are an introvert and prefer just to be in your one corner, then you can turn the dollars down when they start knocking on your doors, Yeah right! That certainly will not be for me.

Let me get you in the mood so you know your list can be endless. Go to Udemy.com and scan through some of the courses that have been listed. Right from bestsellers to newbies, you will realize that there are diverse topics treated. I bet you might even be tempted to enroll in one of them.

Whilst at it, you will get to know the different presentation styles and the different personalities. In short, there is room for everybody and every skill.

1. Now that we have the list, which of these tasks will people be willing to pay for and have a higher market value? For instance, you might be able to know how to cook your local dish very well, but is this dish so popular internationally that it will be sustainable as a business if you produce a course on it? You might also know how to play a certain game as well. Who are the people that will play that game? Do they have money enough to buy a course? If you did the exercise of visiting UDEMY, then you might have also noticed that some are bestsellers in their topics. Was there a particular trend you noticed? That should help you here in shortlisting.

2. Who are you targeting as your customer?

Knowing your ideal student is very important. Are they teenagers, businessmen, IT professionals, mothers, and children? This is because your message will be crafted with them in mind. You will know their frustrations, desires, and their needs so you speak directly to it. This should guide you every step of the way in your course creation process. If your target is young students, some funky way of presentation can be ideal or an intro song can be used to get them in the mood. You cannot do the same for a professional person who wants to learn how to perform well at the negotiation table. When you are able to always differentiate, you will stand out and your students will also love you.

1. Pick the best of topics – for you to attract the needed traffic to your course, your topic should not be broad. It should be specific so that your students can actually pinpoint the benefit or the value they would have added to themselves after finishing it. It should be detailed enough but well outlined so they can follow through without getting confused. For instance, Baking is broad, and even baking cakes is also broad because we have so many types of cakes. Did you know though that there are different variations to preparing chocolate cakes, carrot cakes, or even in decorating cakes? That is, therefore, a better topic to teach than just baking because it tackles the specifics.

1. Now we will take a trip back to UDEMY. This is to validate the topic we want to use. It is to find out how

many courses are related to what you do and if it is viable. You will also get to know how many students have enrolled in those courses. Don't just search with one topic, play around it to get the most of the exercise. This is important because, what use will a course be if after spending your time and money, nobody buys it. Your topic can set you up with the right niche and give you good prices. It is therefore very important to choose your topic well.

1. Validate it again using the tool "Keywords Everywhere". This is a chrome extension and it is a free tool. Download it and install. It will let you know how popular your topic is by giving you the number of times people have searched for those words in a given period. This is also important because we will want to know our potential market outside UDEMY too.

1. Another site we can use for validation of our topic is Youtube. It is a well-known fact that many people visit Youtube when they are searching for videos. We will, therefore, put in our topics and search to see how popular it is.

When checking, try and read the comments that come with it. Your course should address all the concerns raised by people on the various videos put out there.

GATHERING OF INFORMATION FOR OUR CONTENTS
DAY 2 /STEP 2

Your customers know that they could have had all the needed information by searching through the many online platforms. However, information overload sometimes gets them more confused than before. They, therefore, expect you to give them what they are paying for, and that is what you will promise them in your sales and overview videos. You need them to give you positive reviews and ratings, therefore in all your doings, always have their satisfaction in mind. The money should not be the first thing on your mind. It should be the satisfaction of your students.

Luckily for us, we do not have to re-invent the wheel. All, we need to do is to gather the relevant solutions and package them so our students can have value for money. Your students should come out of the course knowing they have added value to themselves in line with what your topic says.

For this to happen let me emphasize this point again - teach something more specific. Students want specific instructions to better a skill or increase their knowledge. That is why they came to you and not to search engines. General information on subjects is all over the internet.

For instance, the topic of Baking is quite broad. However, to be specific, our topic can be How to Bake a Fruitcake. This can even be broken down further with the topic, "How to Bake Fruitcake with Sunflower oil". Let us take workouts, for instance, you cannot have one course that addresses all the many ways to exercise. One size does not fit all. Therefore, you can decide to treat belly exercises for a flatter tummy as one course. Flabby arms elimination or reduction can also be another course for you.

Whilst at it, let us use Day-1 to also gather all images and videos we personally have and will want to include. If we don't have any yet, jot a list of things or demonstrations we will want to include in our course to make it more practical and understanding. We will use these list as a guide during our production

OUTLINE OF THE COURSE

DAY 3 /STEP 3

AT THIS POINT, WE WILL look at all the information gathered and group them according to the order of sequence in your tutorials. For instance, in cake making, you cannot bake before creaming or mixing your ingredients. One comes after the other. In computer assembling or fixing, there are steps to follow, before the final stage. That is how your course should be too. They should be arranged in such a way that it will make logical sense for the student to benefit.

Let's look at a good course outline. This is from how you start your course until you conclude.

    a. Introduction – This should be about 1 minute, 30 seconds to a maximum of 2 minutes, introducing yourself and the course.

    b. Overview of your course – The overview gives a summary of your course and what your student should expect. That should be about 4 minutes. Here you talk about the perceived problem, the myths around it, the mistakes people make, and your solution.

c. Content –here is where your actual teaching begins. Well laid out in a clear and very easy to understand steps, starting from the scratch and progressing till you have given them every needed step as promised. Too many modules will put your students off and might even let them stop the course middle way. Therefore, try to keep the course as short as possible. If it will be too long, try and split it into two. It can be a part one and a part 2. That, of course, will even earn you more money.

d. At this point, some students might be getting confused no matter how simple your approach may be. So give them a video on mistakes to avoid. If you are teaching on Cakes, you know cake mixing can be daunting at times, so alert them on common mistakes and how to avoid it. All skills have avoidable mistakes and your student should be alerted to avoid it. This little thoughtfulness and details will give you good ratings from students.

e. At this point, a student will want to know if he or she is on track. So show a sample or demo of what a successful skill learned should look like. For example, if your tutorial was on website creation, then a demo or picture of a finished website should be shown. If it was on Videography, then a finished video should be shown. Fruit Cupcakes tutorials can show a picture or demo of the finished cakes.

Here you can also request assignments on what you have thought to ensure they understood you.

a. The next step can then be a bonus course related to what you taught them. In my case, my bonus course could be a how-to video on upselling your course or how to successfully make good sales for your online course. It is a course on cupcakes, then a different but short tutorial on a related pastry or how to decorate it with butter frosting should be added as a bonus. The secret here is that it can actually lead the student into your next course by arousing his or her interest. Is that not a win-win situation?

b. Conclusion – Here you thank them once again for enrolling with you and you sell your other courses to them or you upsell this particular one by letting them know you can take them on a one-on-one coaching session. Or where you have blogs, books or youtube channels, you tell them about it. This should be about two minutes. You will also lead them to your website to find downloadable materials and the resources you used. This is where the affiliate sales can be capitalized on for you to make extra sales.

Please note – Conversational tones are preferred these days so let me emphasize it again, be warm in your scripts. Let your students love you because of how you relate to them. It doesn't matter if you live at opposite ends of the world. His or her satisfaction is what will make you a bestseller. We have come this far so we can do it. I have faith in you, should I be worried? No way!

Ok, we have everything laid out now so our work should be easier from now on. You will notice that I did not give you a time frame for the actual content. This is because that will be dependent on your area of specialty and the course you are teaching. Some take time. Others take just about an hour. The beginner courses take a shorter period to cover, whereas the more advanced ones take a bit of time. Whether short or mid-length, the key point here is Quality Delivery and not to bore your students. Too short a course will be seen by your students as a ripoff. Too long a course will sometimes also put your students off and cause them never to finish it. This will give it a bad rating.

CHOOSE A TITLE
DAY 4 / STEP 4

Choose your title carefully – Yes, your title can make or mar all your efforts. People search for information with certain keywords. The blogs and companies that make it to the top in search rankings, study these words and make the most out of it by using them in their titles and write-ups.

This is very important because, without those keywords captured in your title, you will never make it to the front page of Google where all the action is. Ask yourself how many times you have moved to page 2 of Google or any search engine for that matter. There are ways to ensure you have the right words in your titles. There are some keywords that keep on appearing whenever people search for information online especially when you need solutions to fix a problem. I remember the phrase "How to" became an everyday thing for me when I was desperately looking for solutions online to my debt woes.

After "how to", the next common thing to do will be to add the subject in question. These are the keywords that we should watch out for in choosing titles. Any mistake there will let you lose, in spite of all the hard work and research put into your course. Our earlier research on the validation of our course will come handy here. You can also go back to UDEMY and Keys everywhere to check again. Factor the most searched for words in your title to help you in being more visible.

This exercise is important because there is no new thing under the sun and if you want to make it as an online course creator, then you will have to tow the lines of the successful ones. Some courses are charged higher not just because of their content but by the mere title, they are put in a niche that is ready to pay so much for it. People prefer concrete deadlines in titles to challenge them. If they are buying a course on belly reduction, they expect to see for instance – "How to eat your way to Belly reduction in 30 days". Not just how to eat to reduce your belly. We are creating our course in 7 days and that is captured in our title.

Factoring these important cues into your title will place your course at exactly where you want it to be – where your potential student will be when they start searching for courses like yours.

Test the title through a survey. You can do this through the help of the groups and friends you already know who will benefit from your course.

PRODUCTION

DAY 5 /STEP 5

Now we are all set to produce our first online course. Make some noise if you are excited. I will cruise you through it no matter the mode you pick. Why go for the hard way when you can easily get the production done and quickly move on to other things.

With all our tools prepped and in motion, let's begin;

TIME TO PUT OUR COURSE TOGETHER

I must emphasize these points before we begin,

- Keep text simple and short
- Text slide should be easy to read
- Use Big Bold Text
- Sans Serif is a good font style to use
- Limit the slides to one per point
- Use images to make your presentation interesting
- You can use a full screen or half screen

Option 1 – Slides and Voice Over
To edit with Screencast o Matic
There are two options here,

1. You can choose the scripts button on the app.
2. Starting with the titles and points as you have outlined already, you will place them in the templates provided until you get all done. You then choose your microphone from the icon on the screen to start

recording.

3. Each point will be recorded separately so when you finish recording one point, click on next.

4. If you are using your phone, record the audios per sections as you have scripted, then click on the right-hand side, and choose import audio. You can redo or undo with the buttons at the top.

5. Once that is done, you can combine sections to make it one big slide for your screen recording. This can be done by putting your cursor before the first letter of your second section, click backspace, answer yes to the question asked, and you are good to go.

Option 2

1. Prepare Google slides as I showed you earlier and put in a presentation mode. This ensures the best quality when recording.

2. Launch your Screencast o Matic software from their website (Sign up first and choose the Premier or deluxe option, if you have not done that already. Please do not choose the free option). Or if you have done that already, then open the app from your desktop.

3. When you are ready to record your slides, launch the recorder on the app. A dotted black box will appear, on your screen. Drag the sides of it and position it on the Google slides to cover the areas you want to be captured.

4. Choose a preset size to 720p as required by UDEMY

5. 'Narration' enables you to talk over your slides. Click the arrow and choose your microphone. If you will use your phone recorder, record first in the order you created the slides, then upload.

6. Once all is set, press on the record button for it to start recording your presentation.

7. When it finishes recording, click on the blue button. Preview to see if you are satisfied. If not, trash it and record it again. If satisfied, click on done and save.

8. At this stage, you can enhance your recording by clicking on the edit button and then select the tools icon to see the range of effects that can be used. You can add more text, zoom on some portions, add other images, etc.

TO EDIT WITH EASYVSL Software

1. Paste your scripts and add your transitions icon. This will let the software demarcate the slides exactly as you want it to be. I advise that each slide takes only one point or sentence to make reading simpler and not boring.

1. There are many templates to pick from. So out of that, pick the one that best suits the message you want to send across or what you think will appeal to your students. Choose the color, gradient and background image all from the software. You can also upload your custom layout.
2. Upload your audio into the editor and cut out all unwanted parts with their easy to use tools.
3. Save the finalized audio, and sync with the slides.
4. Its intelligence feature will detect your voice and match it to the slides for you.
5. Export into the MP4 format needed. The supported file format for videos is WMV., MP4 and. MOV whereas for slides you must use. PDF file format.

IS THERE ANYTHING EASIER than this? Let me give you one juicy hint with EASYVSL. Do you know you can even choose a voice to read your slides as a voice-over? Yes. Although, I will not recommend that now. This is because your course can funnel into bigger engagements like coaching, seminars, etc., your students will get confused when they talk to you one-on-one.

OPTION 2 – SLIDES WITH videos
Steps for Screencast o Matic

1. Follow steps 1 to 8 as above, then insert your video recording if you have some already from previous demonstrations. If not, after creating your slides, as above, launch the recorder of Screencast o Matic. When it opens, choose both "option". This will enable the screen and the camera you are using. Make sure you have chosen the right microphone and camera by clicking on the respective buttons to select the appropriate one.

1. One important feature with this software is the ability to remove any background and replace it with what you want. It is popularly called the Green Screen. To do this, before you record, click on the preference and click on the remove background. Be sure to sit with your back facing a plain background. That background should not have the same colors as your clothing.

1. Every single thing you need to do, right from recording through to editing is covered under the tutorials that come with the subscription. They are all broken down into the simplest forms for the beginner to use with

ease.

1. When you are done and satisfied with everything, save on your Google drive as an MP4 video for later uploading.

To edit with EasyVSL Software

1. Follow steps 1, 2 and 3 above
2. Then upload the videos recorded with your webcam or phone camera, into the Easyvsl software editor. Edit out all unwanted parts with the easy to use tools and cut them out into the portions you want.
3. Save the final videos
4. Mix and match with the presentations as you go along.
5. Sync
6. Export in the MP4 format needed.

This option is more popular with online courses because it brings a better engagement and connection with your students.

PRE LAUNCH ACTIVITIES

DAY 6 /STEP 6

Now our course is ready, congratulations, we made it this far, and in less than a week, you are a course instructor and a creator now. You can now make the world a better place by providing skills to the many people that are seeking for it but have no time to be in the physical classroom.

It is not over though, let me say this is where the real deal is. Some courses are tagged as bestsellers and others are not because of what happens at this stage. We do not want to just create a course, we want to be amongst the best and have value for what we have invested in. How do we achieve that?

Let's stop to think again, how do we let people know about our course? Yes, we carefully picked out the course name so we can be ranked high on search engines.

We haven't come this far only to get our baby shoved under the carpet. Nope. Our goal is to be noticed, to be taken seriously and to drive traffic to our course with the ultimate aim of making good sales. Well, we need money, but we should not come out as scammers and over-aggressive. So where will we get more sales to make our efforts worthwhile?

We need to gain the attention of our target audience. The good news here is that, on Udemy, we have millions of students willing to learn from us because they have already built the brand for us.

The bad news is that there are many others like you all competing for the same attention.

In order to stand tall and make headway, it is very important to do things that will bring our targets closer. This is the only way that will guarantee our success and move us up to be a bestseller.

TO HELP US DO THAT, there are a few things we will have to do.

Create a Landing Page on UDEMY for your Course.

A landing page is the very first point of call for your potential students. Whether they searched themselves or they followed a lead to be there, the information on your landing page at UDE-MY will help them to decide on enrolling or not. They do this by checking on your course title, course description, and an overview or introduction explaining your course. In this case, how do you get an effective landing page? By learning from the bestsellers. A typical bestsellers page on UDEMY has the following

a. Course Title
b. Subtitle – This explains in a sentence what your course provides
c. The language used
d. Bullet points of some key points in your modules that will excite your students
e. Requirements needed to enroll e.g if special tools are needed by students
f. Description of your course in a few words.
g. Who the course is for
h. Your course contents and duration for each (you can get this info from the recordings done already.

    i. Your profile

    j. Reviews if any

    k. Price of your course (UDEMY will give the range)

Well, the good news is that UDEMY will provide you with the template and you just fill in the details. We know all the above already from our initial outlines so we will give them what we have already prepared.

Udemy promotions.

Like I said earlier on, UDEMY has limits on how much you can charge. Your course can be free to your students for some time just to get ratings or you can charge between 20$ to 200$. They have options for you to promote your course by marketing your course through them to over 15 million students all over the world. They do this through many social media platforms and in order to attract these students, they slash your course down sometimes by over 90%. As a newbie, you will have to accept that so you can gain grounds. And build your audience.

TIME TO LAUNCH

DAY 7 / STEP 7

Now to the most exciting part, LAUNCH LAUNCH LAUNCH. I have good news for you, we are ready to publish for the whole world to see. To do this;

    1. Sign up to UDEMY as an instructor. When you go to udemy.com, click on 'teach on UDEMY'. They will give you the option to sign up with Google or Facebook or

email.

2. Follow all necessary prompts to validate

3. Click on 'TEACH', follow all the prompts to create your title, category, who the course is for, etc. just like you have done earlier (cut and paste)

4. Upload your video.

5. You submit for review and when it is approved (it will definitely if you used all info as I taught you), you are on to make good money.

6. You are then allowed to also upload your intro video or sales video to draw in more traffic.

THE BONUS

For staying till the end, you deserve commendation. To reward you, below are some tips to make you stand out from the crowd.

Build the trust of your students with a little effort.

As a beginner in course creation, we will need to earn some income through enrollments and also to get some good reviews to back us up when our course is published. This is where our friends and followers on social media come in. To get this done, we need to share our course with our friends and families, with the help of our social networks (Instagram, Facebook, LinkedIn, Whatsapp, etc., and at other places where your course will be relevant. This can be done with the sales videos we made since the video attracts more. We should always remember to add a call the action button and link it to our course when we share it.

Once we are well established as a UDEMY instructor, we can gain more by building a platform outside of Udemy to drive our own traffic for our course. This can be done through YouTube channels and many other platforms. More on that in my subsequent books.

Well well well, what can I say? We made it finally Dear, Not only do we have a viable course to sell for good passive income, but we have a well-designed landing page, and a sales video to drive sales.

Wishing you all the best. Please let me know how it goes with this link to my website.

www.simplestepsseries.com

You can also have access to more resources by joining our Facebook page free with this link.

https://web.facebook.com/groups/courseforincome/

THANKS SO MUCH FOR taking this step for believing, it will pay off.

Please don't forget to leave your review. I will love to hear from you.

Happy Course Creation

Best Regards,

Dorcas Ayesu-Boahene

dorcas@simplestepsseries.com

www.simplestepsseries.com[1]

https://web.facebook.com/simplecoursecreation/

Don't miss out!

Visit the website below and you can sign up to receive emails whenever Dorcas Ayesu-Boahene publishes a new book. There's no charge and no obligation.

https://books2read.com/r/B-A-EIZI-UJABB

BOOKS 2 READ

Connecting independent readers to independent writers.

About the Author

Dorcas Ayesu-Boahene has been an entrepreneur for over 23 years now with a specialization in Marketing. She loves mentoring and coaching people to realize their potentials.

She rebranded the Regional branch of a TV Station in Ghana, during her tenure as the Regional Manager, and successfully increased its revenue at that time by over 500%. She was in that position for over 12 years whilst doing other side hustles like creating documentaries and TV commercials for businesses.

She was the first to open a grocery shop solely for kids from 0 to 5 years, in Kumasi (Mega Kids Mart / www.megakidsonline.com).

Read more at https://www.simplestepsseries.com.